ONCE UPON A DREAM

A Wonderland Of Words

Edited By Lynsey Evans

First published in Great Britain in 2024 by:

Young Writers
Est. 1991

Young Writers
Remus House
Coltsfoot Drive
Peterborough
PE2 9BF
Telephone: 01733 890066
Website: www.youngwriters.co.uk

All Rights Reserved
Book Design by Ashley Janson
© Copyright Contributors 2024
Softback ISBN 978-1-83565-846-8
Printed and bound in the UK by BookPrintingUK
Website: www.bookprintinguk.com
YB0607W

FOREWORD

Welcome Reader, to a world of dreams.

For Young Writers' latest competition, we asked our writers to dig deep into their imagination and create a poem that paints a picture of what they dream of, whether it's a make-believe world full of wonder or their aspirations for the future.

The result is this collection of fantastic poetic verse that covers a whole host of different topics. Let your mind fly away with the fairies to explore the sweet joy of candy lands, join in with a game of fantasy football, or you may even catch a glimpse of a unicorn or another mythical creature. Beware though, because even dreamland has dark corners, so you may turn a page and walk into a nightmare!

Whereas the majority of our writers chose to stick to a free verse style, others gave themselves the challenge of other techniques such as acrostics and rhyming couplets. We also gave the writers the option to compose their ideas in a story, so watch out for those narrative pieces too!

Each piece in this collection shows the writers' dedication and imagination – we truly believe that seeing their work in print gives them a well-deserved boost of pride, and inspires them to keep writing, so we hope to see more of their work in the future!

CONTENTS

Ashingdon Primary Academy, Ashingdon

Primrose Coulson (10)	1
Charlie Bradford (10)	2
Charles Kessell (10)	3

Blackwell Primary School, East Grinstead

Chaithra Sreejith Nair (10)	4
Khuspreet Kaur Khonna (9)	5

Brockhampton Primary School, Bringsty

Joshua Morris (7)	6

Derwent Primary School, Derby

Chloe Moyo (11)	7
Folahan Ezekiel Popoola (11)	8
Maisie Redfern (11)	10
Florence Hobday (10)	11
Amelia Evelyn Poole (11)	12
Bradley Heeley (11)	13
Jacob John Price (11)	14
Bella Baker (10)	15
Damian Hurst (11)	16
Byron Reece Fay (11)	18
Aaden Gabriel (10)	19
Serenity Sheldon (11)	20
Lexie Mae Phelps (10)	21
Kade Forster (11)	22
Michael Stone Kalu (11)	23
Mason Barrington (11)	24
Katalina Kulesevicius (11)	25

Efezino Odafe (11)	26
Anton John Bellagoshi (11)	27

Donnington Primary School, Brent

Jessie Hinton (10)	28

Dorrington Academy, Birmingham

Anthonia Obioha (11)	29
Hana Rahim (11)	30
Sara Ebrahim (11)	31
Ehsaan Islam (11)	32
Manal Tunio (11)	33

Harlowbury Primary School, Old Harlow

Maite Santos Leon (8)	34
Sienna Grant (9)	35
Ayat Waqar (9)	36
Hafsa Rizwan (9)	37
Mya Cruse (9)	38
Isaaq Mahiz (9)	39

Hewens Primary School, Hayes

Ekamveer Singh (8)	40
Rashmi Pakeerathan (10)	41
Ethan Hatcher (9)	42
Rui Degun (10)	43
Jansev Khurana (8)	44
Alina Ghaibi (8)	45
Larisa Hedzic (10)	46
Anayah Khan (10)	47

Ukasha Ismail (9)	48
Zayd Kader (8)	49
Himani Khanna (8)	50
Rezon Macwan (9)	51
Varunesh Pakeerathan (8)	52
Guru Degun (8)	53
Lexie Wright (9)	54
Haris Rahimi (9)	55
Jasgun Kaur (10)	56
Cherinah Cole Barrie (9)	57
Aryan Hussain (8)	58
Jacob Harrison (9)	59

Honington Church Of England Voluntary Controlled Primary School, Bury St Edmunds

Hedley Everett (9)	60
Florence Tatum (9)	61
Aliza Edwards (9)	62
Lucien Morgan (9)	63
Jack Buckeridge (9)	64
Oliver Clark (9)	65
Emilia Waugh (9)	66
Daniel Johns (9)	67
Harper Hedges (8)	68
Oscar Doran (8)	69
Arthur Heartford (8)	70
Alfie Cakebread (9)	71

Langdon Academy, East Ham

Amena Rahman (10)	72
Sania Rehman (10)	74
Musfika Islam (10)	75
Praveen Logeswaran (9)	76

Mellers Primary School, Radford

Eyoha Tilahun (10)	77
Rozhin Hamza (10)	78
Maram Elemam	79
Maya Kaur	80

St Alfege With St Peter's CE Primary School, Greenwich

Arinze Njemanze (11)	81
Obinna Ndukwe (11)	82
Bernice Enadeghe (11)	84

St Joseph's RC School, Woodend

Marley-Rose Willoughby (6)	85
Wilhemina Fagbohun (7)	86
Maggie Santeugini (7)	87
Arshika Rawat (7)	88

St Thomas More's Catholic Primary School, Havant

Natalia Borciuch (10)	89
Olly Sparks (9)	90
Enaaya Zeeshan (11)	91
Jill King (11)	92
Jessica Barber (10)	93
Gabe Fry (10)	94
Alice Bates (10)	95
Eden Ross (10)	96
Matthew Dixon (10)	97
Maddison Sutton (10)	98
Millie Wilson (11)	99
Elliott Boyce (9)	100
Anya Gohil (10)	101
Alfie Anderson (9)	102
Dexter Johnson (10)	103
Bella Swales (10)	104
Andrew Mitchell (10), Felix Linto & Freddie	105
Nellie Goudarzi (11)	106
Elsie Stouse (10)	107
Andrew Wardon (10)	108
Caiden Aylett (10)	109
Lenny Tyler (10)	110
Alarna Gomez (10)	111
Niamh Haynes (11)	112
Artur Eva (10)	113

White Meadows Primary School, Wick

Alan Sowa (8)	114
Bethany Fenner (8)	116
Harriette Talman (7)	117
Paige Skinner (8)	118
Lyna Ben Amor (8)	119
Marlie Winter (8)	120
Mylee-Jayne Legge (8)	121
Vanellope Yardley (8)	122
Eliza Cranham (8)	123
Dexter Taylor (8)	124
Jake Blackwell (8)	125
Ruby James (8)	126
Isra Kamali (8)	127
Violet Baker (8)	128
Elise Wheatley (8)	129
Ivy-Grace Patridge (8)	130
Hannah Man (8)	131
Lilly Doyle (8)	132
Kian Wolfe (8)	133
Matylda Beaumont (7)	134
Jacob Elijah Thayre (7)	135
Caelan Barton (8)	136
Nyah Shereni (8)	137
Holly Benson (8)	138
Lewis Ross Hardy (8)	139
Jacob Lucas (8)	140
Siyana Todorova (8)	141
Ivy Martin (8)	142
Ava Misselbrook (8)	143
Ollie Williamson (7)	144
Kaitlyn Akers (8)	145
Albi Taylor (8)	146
Latisha Banson (8)	147
Nova-Grace Harding (7)	148
Ronnie Hodder (8)	149
Logan Lamb-Gardner (8)	150
Junior Kerse (8)	151

William Martin CE Junior School, Harlow

Jesse Wye (9)	152
Jacob Adams (9)	153
Jack Hogg (9)	154
Leo Rees (8)	155
Ajla Hoxha (9)	156
Liban Ahmed (9)	157
Eliana Patti (9)	158
Spencer Matthews (9)	159
Naomi Woodley (9)	160
Max Cuthbert (9)	161
Filip Piziorski (9)	162
Louie Brandle (9)	163
Muhammad Khalid Ibrahim (9)	164
Helena Ingall (9)	165
Ben Hollis (9)	166
Malakai Oderinde (9)	167
Ellie Williamson (8)	168
Stanley Gibb (9)	169
Cavell Brefo-Anum (9)	170
Joseph Didcock (9)	171
George Doyle-Worton (9)	172
Brody Wayman (9)	173
Braxton Findlay (9)	174

Willow Wood Community Primary, Wharton

Ellie-Lou Simpson (10)	175
Damien Durose (10)	176

Wilmslow Preparatory School, Wilmslow

Sophia Davis (9)	177
William Teahan (9)	178
William Lambert (8)	179
Ava Ummat (9)	180
Cailey Li (8)	181
Molly McConville (8)	182

THE CREATIVE WRITING

Time To Dream

Up on the stars,
Leads the way to Mars,
And black sky comes it means it is time to rest,
Dreams are best,

We lay our head on our pillow,
And through the night we dream of willows,
You can dream in your imagination,
And maybe you have a friend named Grason,

As time goes,
Our imagination starts to grow,
Out my window, the moon is dawning,
That means almost morning,

The moon is now dawning,
Now it is morning,
We go and tell Mum and Dad our dreams,
And when the stars are glistening, you know what time it is.

Primrose Coulson (10)
Ashingdon Primary Academy, Ashingdon

The Monkey In The Jungle

The happy monkey with bright, orange eyes,
He just wants to hang in the trees and reach the skies,
Or maybe make a banana pie.

The happy monkey was not so happy today,
People had cut down his tree today.
No tree, no sky, not even a banana pie.

Over the hill, far away Monkey went,
Looking left, looking right, until he found a tree again.
Up on the hill, far away, he found a tree
And climbed to the top and reached the sky,
Whilst of course eating a banana pie.

He was a happy monkey again!

Charlie Bradford (10)
Ashingdon Primary Academy, Ashingdon

The Daydreamer

D uring school, I daydream of space
A nd stars and planets, it's a wonderful place
Y ou jump and you twirl, free as the stars
D iscovery awaits as you zoom by Mars
R e-entering orbit, you fall at supersonic speed
E arth waiting below, taking the lead
A t once, I'm back in my chair
M iss tells me I should have a care
E ach day I dream about space
R ocketing to Mars, I might find an alien race.

Charles Kessell (10)
Ashingdon Primary Academy, Ashingdon

Royal Fairy Dancers

I hear a twinkle in the night sky
As the royal fairy dancers pass by
Swirling and twirling through the night
Whilst the sky is really quiet
My heart thumps as I see the bioluminescent lights
Yes, I saw them with my own eyes
They come from a world beyond
To create a special bond
They leave a glowing trail
But by day, the lights always fail.

Chaithra Sreejith Nair (10)
Blackwell Primary School, East Grinstead

Royal Flying Dancers

In my dreams every night
I hear a twinkle as they take flight
Dance, the river is there to rise
Dance, touch me and close your eyes
One by one they pass me by
In the shining, bright, beautiful sky
A twirl makes you want to dance
How about we give you a chance
But sadly, they just disappear
For now, perhaps next year.

Khuspreet Kaur Khonna (9)
Blackwell Primary School, East Grinstead

Once Upon A Dream

Every night, I dream of becoming a Red Dino Fury Power Ranger.
Every day will be full of adventure and lots of danger.
All my equipment, which includes my blazing dino key and Morpher
Will help me along the way with my superpower.
There will be so much to practise, I may not have time for a shower.
My arch enemy, Void Knight, I am ready for a fight.
When he calls for his henchmen and says, "Destroy them all."
Me (Zayto Dino Fury) will link to Morphin' Grid
Blazing dino key ready, blazing battle armour
And save the world from my enemies.

Joshua Morris (7)
Brockhampton Primary School, Bringsty

It May Seem Like A School But In My World, It's A Prison

As the day closes,
I get dismissed from my cell,
Homework is looming and discipline if I delay,
But worst of all, it has to be done by today!

We drive teachers mad,
It makes us feel glad,
In my world, it is a prison,
It may seem like school,
Yet inside, it's the complete opposite.
Teachers watching my every move!

It may seem like I'm over-exaggerating,
But trust me, I'm not,
I can't be late, I need to escape!

Escaping feels like freedom,
But believe me when I say, it's impossible,
When all eyes are on me,
As I wake up from my dream, I was already in trouble!
I didn't do my homework so back I go to my cell.

Chloe Moyo (11)
Derwent Primary School, Derby

The House And Matt

Ding-dong went the clock
As the house went flashing by
With a rusty black window
Filled with animals like black widows
A vampire went zoom
As the clouds of blue

He went in, *ding-ding*
As the house went dark
A tree danced from the ground
As he was going around
His heart was beating fast
And his brain was getting a blast

He went into the house
And he saw a small mouse
An owl began to cry as the house moved by
The house was as big as Earth
As he felt he was giving birth
He saw a huge man
Like the size of a giant can

The man squashed him to death
As he said goodbye, Earth
He woke up and realised it was a dream
As he let out a sigh of relief.

Folahan Ezekiel Popoola (11)
Derwent Primary School, Derby

Sweetland Fun

It's all going fine in Sweetland
The sky, as pink as candyfloss
The floor, covered in freeze-dried sweets
Candyfloss melts below our feet
As the world shakes
The dogs begin to bark
As the night grows dark

The people are screaming, hip hooray
All the fun starts today
The clouds screaming, oh my
And the birds begin to sigh
They always do it at this time
And I always wonder why

As far as I knew
The time had flew
I was in a UFO
With aliens, I know
Flying away to Mexico.

Maisie Redfern (11)
Derwent Primary School, Derby

Sparkle Glitter Land

Sparkling stars up in the sky
Lollipop trees waving goodbye
Grass glittering on my bare feet
Making an appointment for a fairy to meet
Showing the fairy around so she can take over the world
The sparkling river made out of sapphires
Crossing over the chocolate bridge on fire
Passing a tall candy cane standing proud
Pop, whistle, sprinkle, fireworks so loud
Marshmallow butterflies flutter by
Candyfloss bunnies hop and cry
A big, round, red, sparkly button in sight
Press it now to reveal the snow's might.

Florence Hobday (10)
Derwent Primary School, Derby

School Pool Day

I wake up in the morning
And I hear my dad snoring
Today I say hooray
Because it's school pool day
I look outside my window
And see flowers as colourful as the rainbow
I can hear kids playing
And the trees swaying
I walk to school
And I see the pool
Sitting on the floor as quiet as a mouse
The pool is up
The kids are playing
If I look up to the sky
You'll hear me saying
"Don't splash me, I'm not playing"
Today I say hooray
Because it's school pool day.

Amelia Evelyn Poole (11)
Derwent Primary School, Derby

Untitled

I started by fast falling through the blue sky
Chocolate clouds and gummy birds zoomed quickly by

A wise book loudly told me to have a good look
Multicoloured Skittle grass was a carpet for the bourbon biscuit castle

Strawberry lollipops were handed to me
By the wise book who lived in the deep sweet sea

A massive giant chased after the trees
Throwing lollipops in his mouth to stop his eating mayhem

The giant stopped and said,
"Wake up, you're dreaming in bed."

Bradley Heeley (11)
Derwent Primary School, Derby

The Escape

I wake up in a dream
Like Mr Bean
A broken spaceship to try and get home
A hermit crab named Hermi, with a dome

Hermi says he has a way
But it has a price to pay
We have to climb to the top
And there's a Pritt Stick man to try and stop
So put up a fight
Or you will have a fright

So I climb to the top
And hunger consumes me
Beating Pritt Stick man
We run to the spaceship parts
And repair them
And I go home with Hermi and his dome.

Jacob John Price (11)
Derwent Primary School, Derby

Bad Dreams

Standing there, in a blood-red corridor,
Standing there, whispering,
I want more,
I talk to my friend, then my unicorn,
We glance and see a shadow appearing,
He comes closer and soon, he is here!

Twin girls holding hands,
Walk near the hot sand,
Behind me is a boy, he has a bright toy,
He smiles and laughs with delight.

I say to myself, "It's a dream."
But then we hear a scream!
I wake up and realise
It was nothing but imaginary.

Bella Baker (10)
Derwent Primary School, Derby

The Haunted Circus

The haunted, creepy
Circus woke up
In October and then
A pitbull came
Out of a pit.

Then it let out
A roar and let out
A boar then the
Clown said, "I
Will give you a
Fright if you
Don't give fight."

I named the
Dog Bully
Then a clown
Started to
Clown around.

Then I gave
It a fight then
I got a knife

Which was a sharp
Sword then I
Put it through
Its skull.

Damian Hurst (11)
Derwent Primary School, Derby

Sweetland

Upside down in Sweetland,
A pond with melted Jolly Ranchers,
The sky made out of fluffy marshmallows,
As the earth trembled,
When bad luck ended.

Kade and Damian forever moaned,
In the fountain, Damian goes,
Up and down,
In and out.

The sky was covered in clouds,
Robins cheeped at our feet,
The clock screamed tick-tock,
As the time went flying by,
The clouds screamed, "Oh my",
As the birds began to cry.

Byron Reece Fay (11)
Derwent Primary School, Derby

My Dreamworld

My house is made of gold
With rubies that are cold
Doughy doors
With jelly floors
Popcorn eaten with toffee
When I sip my coffee

Back garden of broccoli trees
Little yellow ducks, not to tease
Spinach grass
With ants that pass
A rockpool
Not for a fool

I am cool at school
A great learning tool
I am an easy model
No need to yodel
No need to frown
Or turn your happiness upside down.

Aaden Gabriel (10)
Derwent Primary School, Derby

My Nightmare

I wake up every night
Screaming from fright
I wake up in a room
Red and black with multiple terrifying booms

"It's time to go to sleep,"
My mother says, then I lie there and weep
I'm sorry, Mum, I'm just not tired
So every day, I wake up feeling wired!

This room terrifies me
I can't sleep, can you not see?
This room is too scary
Every morning, I wake up wary.

Serenity Sheldon (11)
Derwent Primary School, Derby

Maisie's House

In the house, the sky gleams like a diamond.
Floors are covered in silky grass,
Maisie's house, hot like a sauna.
The dog begins to bark
As the night grows dark.

Birds chirp in the sky,
The pool comes alive, go have a dip!
At this time, this is a never-ending friendship.

The house is shaking,
Everyone is happy,
Everyone is watching us
While we walk down the valley.

Lexie Mae Phelps (10)
Derwent Primary School, Derby

A Weird Dream

I wish, I wish, Kade went on a trip
My T-shirt had a big rip

The sweets glowed, the moon spoke
The stars brightened, my eyes closed

My toes grew, my brain knew
I need a clue to find my way back into the real world

The clouds were like marshmallows
The sky was as bright as the sea
Spain was as exciting as it could be
I couldn't believe this was all just a dream!

Kade Forster (11)
Derwent Primary School, Derby

A Day With Marcus Rashford At Old Trafford

Into the stadium, I walk
With the manager, I talk
Marcus Rashford I meet
While standing on my feet
I get signed into the club
Cheering for joy
Me and Rashford play a match
Nutmegging him to Bradford
I score goals that are bold
I feel amazed running down the wing
Scoring goals that go ping
I score a wonderful header that wins the game
Every night my dreams are the same.

Michael Stone Kalu (11)
Derwent Primary School, Derby

Chicken Nugget

C rispy like wood,
H ow good is that?
I 've been,
C ruelly
K icked out of McDonald's,
E ven though my future is ruined,
N ever ever will I give up.

N uggets are my dream.
U are so mean!
G iant as a house.
G olden like the sand.
E njoy the last bite.
T he end.

Mason Barrington (11)
Derwent Primary School, Derby

Nightmares

Alone at home
No one seems to be known
Hoping to survive
Trying to hide
Shadows are alive
People don't lie
Somehow frightened
My fists tightened
The luminous moon
Setting a mood

Nightmares
Like dark demons
Stealing your soul
The dead are awakening
Roars and groans
Praying to be silent.

Katalina Kulesevicius (11)
Derwent Primary School, Derby

Teleport Into Fortnite

My, my, this mansion is as enormous as a T-rex
What a surprise, the mansion is made
Of V-Bucks card floors, diamond windows
Gold walls and a money door
Who could own this marvellous mysterious mansion?
I saw swirly red trees everywhere
Suddenly, I heard multiple gunshots. *Bang!*
Will I be killed or was it just a drill?

Efezino Odafe (11)
Derwent Primary School, Derby

Dream Football Match

In my dream
I'm in a football team
Scoring goals
Every game
Standing straight and tall
Focusing on the ball
I hit the ball with my boot
I celebrate my shot
Quickly I run
In to the fans.

Anton John Bellagoshi (11)
Derwent Primary School, Derby

In My Dreams...

In my dreams every night,
Unicorns fly high and bright.
Luscious hair and rainbow vomit everywhere,
Flying high without a care,
With sparkles in her hair.

Two by two, they pass in the colourful sparkling sky.
The head unicorn rears up above the roof,
Shooting sparkles out of his hooves.
If you want to be like the unicorn,
Just remember, imagination can take you everywhere.

Jessie Hinton (10)
Donnington Primary School, Brent

Nightmares

Nightmares can be full of many things.
Sometimes you can hear screams so loud it makes your ears ring!
They always come once a night,
To try and give you a giant fright!
You try to escape but all you see is smoke,
Which leaves you hoping it's all a joke!
Nightmares fill your head with dread,
That shake you awake so you find yourself in bed!
Some things in nightmares are always creeping around,
And soon you find out it's a very scary clown.
You pinch yourself to hope you wake up from your nightmare,
But when you wake up in bed,
Remember you've always been there!

Anthonia Obioha (11)
Dorrington Academy, Birmingham

The Time I Was Forced To Write A Rhyme

Once upon a time,
I was stuck at school, forced to write a rhyme,
It was as though I had committed a crime,
I felt like I was eating lemons and limes,
My stomach churns,
As another page turns,
Inside me, everything burns,
Whilst my foolish self learns,
This is everything but real,
I feel like I might throw up my most recent meal,
The sky is not dark, but teal,
I might curl up into a ball, hiding what I truly feel,
I look around to see I'm safe in my bed,
And I think I'm crazy, it was all in my head...

Hana Rahim (11)
Dorrington Academy, Birmingham

A Colourful Explosion

I dreamt of...
Explosions of joy conquering the pitch-black sky
They made the moon shine even more brightly
Sweet-smelling flowers filling the air
Colours bursting in the sky, spreading happiness
Masterpieces on a plain black canvas
Paint being vibrant, birds circling the sky
Sparklers exploding into the moonlight
I witnessed glistening sparkles
Explosions of glass shattering

Fluttering like butterflies
Dancing like tornadoes
Colouring patterns in the sky
Blooming like blossom
Hiding behind the clouds
That was the amazing, spectacular dream.

Sara Ebrahim (11)
Dorrington Academy, Birmingham

Clowns

C olours are exploding everywhere, like confetti
L et's hope I'm not scared of blood
O rders of demonic clowns are chasing me like a fleet of zombies
W andering around in the wasteland, trying to escape, I see the fleet hunting for humans, me
N ightmares don't leave, they never will
S uddenly, I'm at home in bed!

Ehsaan Islam (11)
Dorrington Academy, Birmingham

Fantasy

F ar away, in the land of magic,
A lot goes on, some things fun, some things tragic,
N ice things, like lollipops or sweets,
T hough sometimes, things aren't as nice as treats,
A round the world, you could go,
S inging and laughing - it's all in your head,
Y ou realise, suddenly, you're still in bed!

Manal Tunio (11)
Dorrington Academy, Birmingham

My Dream

My dream starts with me coming back from school on a bus when suddenly I'm in front of the house. My house. A baby opens the door for me. I don't know how, but I am calling him Dudu.

I take off my shoes, my shoes are really not nice. When I open the second door, my mum is singing different music. When I do my homework, the baby, Dudu, is calling me Tete. He was saying that I should give one present to him. The present was a phone case. The case, I really like it, but I've given it to him.

The day after, I am really sad that I've given the case to the baby, Dudu, and I am thinking of a plan to take the case back again. My plan is to put a zip line at the end of the baby's room, and I am finally doing the plan. First, I slide on the zip line, and when I'm in the baby's room, I take the phone case and put another one for him.

After my dream, I wake up.

Maite Santos Leon (8)
Harlowbury Primary School, Old Harlow

Winter Wonderland

You wonder why it's cold,
Well because it's always bold,
Welcome to the Wonderland,
On the other hand, it is a Winterland,
Where it's all the same,
I wonder what you can tame.

First, here is the polar bear,
He can always hear,
Secondly, here is the penguin,
He's so cute, that he has a mute,
Thirdly, there's a snow owl, who can hunt,
I will choose all of them because they're in my dream.

This is my favourite dreamland, being with my friends,
I like the snow dreamland, my dream is the best,
All I like is to rest!
I wonder what is going to happen in my dream next,
I will always talk about my dream.

Sienna Grant (9)
Harlowbury Primary School, Old Harlow

My Dream Life

Rainbow, rainbow here I come
Fairies flying in the sun
Unicorn, unicorn passing me by with your fluffy tail in the night sky

In my dream, every night
Space horses fly with colours bright

Nothing turned up on this strange land I see
I take a step backwards as scared as I can be
Dancing left and dancing right
All I see is something
How did I get here and how did I get there?
I hope this is just a scary fate
Something is moving
It's creeping me out
Nothing to fear
It's not frightening
You don't be scared, 'cause I am here.

Ayat Waqar (9)
Harlowbury Primary School, Old Harlow

Running Rats

R unning rats, here and there
U p and down, yet everywhere,
N othing to fear from... hope so, I'm right!
N othing should give me a dreadful fright!
I 'm starting to feel anxious, nowhere to go,
N othing to fear from and nothing to show,
G etting scared, I think, I might cry,

R unning rats, I hope I won't have to say bye!
A round I go, shouting for help,
T hinking about what will happen if I start to yelp!

Hafsa Rizwan (9)
Harlowbury Primary School, Old Harlow

Space Cats!

Every night, me and best friend see Space Cats
Shining ever so bright
We find it hard to sleep at night.
The Space Cats help us sleep
We don't make a peep
When they're here with us.
Me and my best friend love it when they come
But not that much, when it's done.
We see the Space Cats every night
Shining ever so bright.
See you tomorrow night.

Mya Cruse (9)
Harlowbury Primary School, Old Harlow

Life Of A Stray

Once, in a dream, I was left on the streets,
Looking for some meaty treats.
One day, I met some teens,
They were very mean.
I walked away,
It felt like another unlucky day.
Soon, I met another cat,
I asked if we could be friends.
They said yes! Hooray!
This is how my story ends.

Oh, yeah, if you find me, bring me meaty treats!

Isaaq Mahiz (9)
Harlowbury Primary School, Old Harlow

The Dark Secret Of The 9th Planet Existing

Once, it was a quiet, nice and really sunny day. A good day to go and explore, but where? Acting funny, the sun was, through the day, so I was checking the news. Looking at the ninth planet and asking Elon to get the fuse ready, we were going there, so let's get our friends and let's get in the Tesla and go to the next possible land. We got an astronaut, Elon Musk, a footballer and a wizard.

We went and somehow found dinosaurs. We pet one, feeling already tired and annoyed from this place. I saw a Kraken in the sea, hearing snaps everywhere, going to check it. It picked everyone up but we weren't getting hurt.

We were going to go back but we got lost. We had to hide the dinosaur. He could fly, but not so high.

Ekamveer Singh (8)
Hewens Primary School, Hayes

Is This It?

One day, as Rashmi went to play, she wondered,
"Could I find out the meaning of life today?"
So, she discovered a way to make it possible,
But it was a very tricky obstacle.
Then, she entered a time machine,
To make sure all her questions were seen.
All of a sudden, a person appeared, who was very well-dressed, saw me and had something to confess.
"Rashmi! Ahh!" filled the air,
Turns out that was *me* who had found out the meaning of life in the future.
And I was handed a note and shipped away, somewhere with a boat,
And then I saw what it said...
'This note must not be shared.'

...

Rashmi Pakeerathan (10)
Hewens Primary School, Hayes

Teachers!

All teachers, big and small
The one student, they look at and call
As I stand in front of the whole school
"Good morning, Sir," echoes in the room
After a while, we are in the classroom
Teaching maths and English too
With all the tables straight
Soon enough, it will be break
After break, you will see we go and play, and learn PSHE
After that, it is lunch
We have a healthy lunch
After lunch, fresh as daisies
Ready for PE, no one's lazy
Now that the time has approached, half-past three
I can grab myself a cup of tea
I can mark these papers in privacy.

Ethan Hatcher (9)
Hewens Primary School, Hayes

Once Upon A Dream

I believed my mum was queen, my father was king and I was a princess!
The whole world was full of endless possibilities.
Once upon a dream, I could fly to the moon.
Once upon a dream, I could jump on clouds and have candyfloss for breakfast!
And when I closed my eyes my dreams could go on forever.
I could sing on stage in front of a crowd of people.
It was a cruel summer next to Taylor Swift.
And ate loads of chocolate with Willy Wonka himself!
In my dreams, I could be who I wanted.
My dreams gave me hope.
My dreams gave me power.
My dreams could take me anywhere.

Rui Degun (10)
Hewens Primary School, Hayes

The Kid Who Turned Gold

One night, under the light, it was 12:45pm on September 15th, 1989. The royal family was walking in a hallway made of gold. It was dark until the girl shouted, "Help, the guy has turned gold!" And the worst part was, it was next to mould! How crazy is that? Feeling cold. He was very bold.
Chaos! Lots of chaos. *Bang! Crash!* Thunder boomed. A gold bar was picked up by the servant. "Dinner!" said the girl. The boy started moving as gold but on the ground, it was cracked. It broke. The cat was being stroked. The kid was invisible but lots of gold bars were on the ground!

Jansev Khurana (8)
Hewens Primary School, Hayes

A Night Of A Lifetime

Every night in my dreams,
Lies a wonderland not to be seen,
People flying, no one lying,
Every joy around the land,
People smile, people laugh,
And dance around in the aftermath

In this dream not to be seen,
Look around for the next full moon,
When flowers bloom,
Below the moon,
Look at the waterfall,
By the cave of a maze,
And look beyond the sudden waves,
Twists and turns around it all

So do you see the waterfall?
If you do, this is a clue,
For a path beyond this dream.

Alina Ghaibi (8)
Hewens Primary School, Hayes

Spiders

As I sleep comfy in my bed,
Suddenly I'm filled with dread,
Why Larisa you may ask,
It's my worst nightmare alas,
As others dream of unicorns and famous writers,
My dreams are of spooky and scary spiders,
Crawling on my bedroom wall,
Why is it they never fall?
Hanging from a silky thread,
Dangling up above my head,
My heart feels like it's filled with lead,
But he's not moving... is he dead?
And just as I'm about to scream,
I woke up, it was just a dream.

Larisa Hedzic (10)
Hewens Primary School, Hayes

The Forest

T he trees swish and sway around me
H orrible, eerie sounds follow me
E ventually, I hear something rustling in the bushes

F uriously, a huge monster with one eye chases me
O n his blood-crusted lips, there are purple lumps
R unning like Usain Bolt, its eyes start glowing
E verywhere I look are trees surrounding me
S tars in the sky are the only light source I have
T hen, I wake to the sound of my alarm, finding out I am safe at home!

Anayah Khan (10)
Hewens Primary School, Hayes

Monsters Realm

In the land of dreams, where shadows play
Monsters lurk at night they say
With claws and fangs, they come to fright
But in my dreams, I'll hold on tight.

Beneath my covers snug and warm
I'll weather any monstrous storm
With courage deep within my chest
I'll face them down, I'll be my best!

Though darkness falls and fears may creep
In my dreams, I will never weep
For when the morning light does gleam
Monsters vanish, just a dream.

Ukasha Ismail (9)
Hewens Primary School, Hayes

Adventure

A s I lie down to sleep
D rifting off into the world of dreams
V arious wonders to be seen
E very night it's something new
N o limits to what I can be
T ravelling through time, flying through space or being a snail in a slow-paced race
U nlocking mysteries within my mind
R eality and time are no longer mine
E very morning when I wake, I hope to remember the dreams I make.

Zayd Kader (8)
Hewens Primary School, Hayes

My Dream Fairy

In my dream
All I could hear was a scream
So clear and loud
Like a bursting cloud

It made me nervous, with no one to calm
A fairy appeared with all the charm
With a magic wand, riding a unicorn
She smiled at me and my fear was gone

I got a gift from her
A wonderful friend for life, I call her my mother
She's there by my side
And at bedtime, she sings me lullabies.

Himani Khanna (8)
Hewens Primary School, Hayes

The Worry Of Dreams

When I go to sleep
A world of imagination crawls over my head
I dream of anything
I taste a candy bar
I built the world of dreams
People thank me
I gift them my dreams
So I make nightmares
But something dreadful happened
Nightmares took over
So we fought over
And dreams won again
So I stayed still
At least I thought so...

Rezon Macwan (9)
Hewens Primary School, Hayes

The Footballer

Varunesh decided to play football, but during the match, a portal opened up, and he got sucked inside! Then, a footballer, Cristiano Ronaldo, said, "Why don't I take you for a ride?"
"Yes, yes, yes!" he replied.
All of a sudden, they went through spirals and saw Ronaldo's life when he was a kid, which was information made to be hid.

Varunesh Pakeerathan (8)
Hewens Primary School, Hayes

A Dream

When I dream, I can see Anfield,
A giant pitch, beaming lights and a crowd of supporters.
My debut for Liverpool.
Those who played before me - Salah, Virgil, Mac Allister and Gakpo.
The stars with amazing skills.
One day.
One dream.
A chance of a lifetime.
A moment to leave my mark, a dream that I hope becomes a reality.

Guru Degun (8)
Hewens Primary School, Hayes

The Dance Group

Dancers fly every night,
Yes, they do it without a fright,
They pass by me every day,
Their competition is in May,
I like dancing, I hope you do too,
The crowd never says boo,
I will dance forever with my group,
When I'm cold, I will drink soup,
My group supports me,
One of my friends is called Lee.

Lexie Wright (9)
Hewens Primary School, Hayes

Marvellous Mbappé

Mbappé thought he was in space,
But he just had a lot of pace.
Then, he ran into the box
Like a sneaky fox.

After, he got his boots
Ready to shoot,
It went in the top bins
Just like he was striking garbage bins.

The crowd went wild
Like they were in the wild!

Haris Rahimi (9)
Hewens Primary School, Hayes

The Royalty

R iches and gold they all have
O utstanding family in each and every way
Y oung and youthful children they have
A mazing gifts they all had around
L oving, funny there is too much to say
T he lovely parades they create
Y ummy food they enjoy before bed.

Jasgun Kaur (10)
Hewens Primary School, Hayes

I Can Be An Astronaut

One night sky is so blue,
I can be an astronaut just like you,
Floating in the vast sky,
Gazing at the mesmerising stars with my heroes,
I am proud of,
I can be an astronaut,
Just like you,
I have potential,
No astronaut can be like me,
I have a dream.

Cherinah Cole Barrie (9)
Hewens Primary School, Hayes

The Ferocious Monster

When I go to sleep,
I will never peep,
There is something under my bed,
Or it could be over my head,
It could be a ferocious monster,
That can be stronger than a hunter,
Is the monster going to scare me?
I'll have to wait and see.

Aryan Hussain (8)
Hewens Primary School, Hayes

Fantastic Football

Football is a sport and a really good one too,
It keeps you really fit and it's fun to play with your friends too,
You can play it in the park and in the school playground too,
I really love football and you should give it a try too...

Jacob Harrison (9)
Hewens Primary School, Hayes

The Time Traveller's Dream

Once upon a dream, a boy called Tim was walking in the dark. Tim was obsessed with time travel. He had been walking when *whoosh* a blue box appeared out of nowhere and a man, quite skinny, said, "Hi, I'm the Doctor, come in. You know, we can go to Hogwarts."
"Okay."
"Here we are."
"Wow!"
"Hi, I'm Harry."
"Hermione."
"Ron."
"Yes, yes, let's go in the box."
"Okay, we're in Isla Nublar. Dinosaurs!"
"Let her come in. Hermione!"
"Let's go."
"Hi, I'm Bravestone."
"Hi, I'm Captain Jack Sparrow."
"Hi, I'm Indiana Jones."
"Hi, I'm Hulk."
"Ah, back home. 3,2,1..."
"Wake up, Tim."
"Ah, I'm awake."
"Tim, breakfast!"

Hedley Everett (9)
Honington Church Of England Voluntary Controlled Primary School, Bury St Edmunds

My Anything Can Happen Land

In my dreams, I see fairies, wizards, unicorns and more,
In my dreams dinosaurs are real,
Monsters lurk about in every step,
Dragons rule the skies and pirates rule the seas,
It's easy to get lost, just follow the path and you'll be safe.

In my dream, the sky is emerald green while the floor glitters and gleams,
It shines throughout the land whilst adventure calls,
I dream sweet dreams but not like this, the stream turns upside down.

I take a step forward as nervous as can be,
What is this place? I want to go home,
But wait I catch a glimpse in my eye, I see a unicorn as I pass by,
Suddenly I wake up, is it over? It was the best,
I can't wait for tomorrow, wonder what I will do next.

Florence Tatum (9)
Honington Church Of England Voluntary Controlled Primary School, Bury St Edmunds

The Nightmare In Hollywood

Once in a dream,
I went to bed and I woke up in New York,
I was a former dancer, I was performing in Hollywood that day,
Suddenly my mum called me,
It was time to go, I hopped in the car,
When out of nowhere,
A big cloud of darkness flew over me,
I started the car and drove off,
Finally, I had arrived,
I hopped out of the car,
Suddenly there was a big dragon,
He landed right in front of me,
I felt scared,
But I remembered I have superpowers,
So I tased the dragon until he collapsed,
It was time to go after the show, I walked out to my car,
Suddenly loads and loads of monsters appeared,
I was so scared,
I woke up in the morning horrified.

Aliza Edwards (9)
Honington Church Of England Voluntary Controlled Primary School, Bury St Edmunds

An Undiscovered World

In one dream, I was walking with my friend,
And then a shiny portal appeared in front of us,
In hopes we'd be fine, we jumped in,
And saw a new world coming.

We were in. We saw purple grass and radiant trees too,
Also, green cows were shouting, "Moo!"
We walked around to see more,
And then we saw these winged creatures,
Dragons maybe?
They had multicoloured wings and bodies,
They were flying with a huge roar!
They also slept in an unusual way,
Curled up into a ball,
But they were friendly, too.

Soon, the portal started to close,
And we ran back,
We went from dragons to green cows,
To the portal, then,
I was back at home, and it was all a dream.

Lucien Morgan (9)
Honington Church Of England Voluntary Controlled Primary School, Bury St Edmunds

My Dream House

I dream of my dream house as a castle
With brick walls all around
And the strongest modern door
With riches galore.

I walk down hallways and hallways
And I go down them always
With pictures that move and stare
And they always sit on a chair.

With colossal living rooms as big as tombs
With food stacked on food in my living rooms.

And my supreme bedroom
With lots of trees abloom
The fire crackling with laughter and my fluffy
Pillow like a cloud
I rest my head upon it
I awake from my dream.

Jack Buckeridge (9)
Honington Church Of England Voluntary Controlled Primary School, Bury St Edmunds

Gaming Dreams

G aming is the best
A rt of War is really good
M inecraft is the best mining game ever
I nfinity War is very, very good
N intendo games are very nice
G alaxy Warriors is really cool

I gloo Escape is pretty, pretty cool
S tar Wars is the best in the world

F ortnite is the best game ever
U nspeakable is the best YouTuber
N injago Lego.

Oliver Clark (9)
Honington Church Of England Voluntary Controlled Primary School, Bury St Edmunds

Dreams

D reams make people happy and make them feel warm inside and make people
R emember that if you keep dreaming something might come true
E ven dreaming makes you you. If you didn't have it you wouldn't be you now, and dreams are
A wesome because you can have scary dreams and happy dreams
M aybe you can make other's dreams come true too
S o put your amazing brain on and dream big dreams.

Emilia Waugh (9)
Honington Church Of England Voluntary Controlled Primary School, Bury St Edmunds

Space Journey

Here I am on Earth.
In my bed on Earth.
Today I'll figure out what I'm worth.
One night I fell asleep and woke up in space.
It was a peculiar place.
I realised I was floating in zero gravity.
I thought I was in captivity.
I was right.
I was floating towards a black hole.
Now, they say in space nobody can hear you scream.
Aaarghh!
I had fallen into that black nothingness of a black hole.

Daniel Johns (9)
Honington Church Of England Voluntary Controlled Primary School, Bury St Edmunds

A Bad Dream In The Night

N ight in the mist of the moon.
I dream of monsters and
G hosts, haunting my dreams.
H ave… I been here before?
T ime after time, my dreams vanish and
M y nightmares appear.
A world of fright, spiders and fatal
R eality. Clowns, monsters and horror
E at all the good dreams, leaving me in sorrow.

Harper Hedges (8)
Honington Church Of England Voluntary Controlled Primary School, Bury St Edmunds

Dreamiest Dreams

D ogs running all around your house
R hinos going for a morning jog past your house
E ggs dancing and standing on your head
A nimals coming in for lots of cuddles
M onsters running down the road
S uperheroes whizzing through the night sky.

Oscar Doran (8)
Honington Church Of England Voluntary Controlled Primary School, Bury St Edmunds

I Slept On And On In The Night

I slept on and on in the night.
Dreaming that I was in flight.
I landed on the moon.
I made a room by noon.
I woke up in the morning,
Just as the day was dawning.
I fell into a black hole.
I felt cold.
It was there I met him,
Just there.

Arthur Heartford (8)
Honington Church Of England Voluntary Controlled Primary School, Bury St Edmunds

The Galaxy Of Galaxies

The Yum Yum Galaxy
Blue, purple and dark blue
Swirling round like a tornado
Alfie's base that's made out of Galaxy blocks
Stars and blaze powder
He had a dog called Coby
They loved swimming in space
With an alien called Dethyon.

Alfie Cakebread (9)
Honington Church Of England Voluntary Controlled Primary School, Bury St Edmunds

Triple Dream Trouble

Once I went to the market
To buy some fish
I chose the best fish
To eat for my dish
But then it opened its mouth
And began to talk
It wanted to get out
Go away and walk
Suddenly I see a dragon in the sky
Flying high and then higher
It looks down at me
And breathes a great jet of fire.

I open my eyes
And I can see
A great underwater world
I'm at the bottom of the sea
There! There's a shark
Or is it a bee?
I have no idea
But it's coming after me!

I swim for my life
As the shark bee gives chase

I look to the surface
And pick up my pace
The shark bee shouts out
"Hey, come back here!"
I look back at the creature
It's getting very near.

One last burst of speed
I quickly look back
Just as the shark bee swallows me whole
And it all turns to black.

I open my eyes once more
Just in time to see
A great, big monkey
Soaring past a tree.

Flying monkeys
As fast as can be
High above the treetops
One looks down at me

That particular sight
Was too much to comprehend
I leap out of bed
And my dream comes to an end.

Amena Rahman (10)
Langdon Academy, East Ham

Bones In The Stones

Hurry, hurry
It's time to scurry
Goblins and bats
Ghosts and black cats
Watch out for the bones
They are lying in the stones
Life is short, and
I've shortened mine
Being a skeleton isn't so easy
When wintertime comes
And the weather gets freezy
I shake and I rattle
Click, clickety clock
Click, clickety click
Somebody throw me an overcoat
Bones, bones hard and strong
All connected so nothing goes wrong
My bones help me out
My bones help my body about
Bony, bony, bony bones
With nothing in-between
Up and down and all around
They march on the streets all about.

Sania Rehman (10)
Langdon Academy, East Ham

Shooting Space

Now I'm in a world full of light,
But all I can see is the stars shining bright.
I stood alone,
Lost in space,
Gazing up lazily,
Into lightness around.
I made a wish and hoped it would find the truth,
For the sad soul to be cleansed and soothed.
That smile to shine as bright as the moon,
Which shines in tonight's sky as the daylight looms.
I pinched myself...
Aaahh!
I woke up, it was all a dream...
Now I lie there in my bed staring into space!

Musfika Islam (10)
Langdon Academy, East Ham

My Dark Dream

I put one foot in the dark,
Realising what fears I could pass by.
Thinking that a shark had bitten away all my good enthusiasm,
And all that was left was fear.
I was near some ominous figure,
I gasped with petrifying thoughts.
Could it be a villain or a monster?
Without a second thought, I headed over to the shadow.
Biting my nails about 1,000 times,
I could see the monster.
But I was as courageous as can be,
Suddenly, I woke up to see it was all a dream.

Praveen Logeswaran (9)
Langdon Academy, East Ham

Flying Ballerina

Little ballerina dance for me,
A delightful scene for anyone to see,
Prancing and dancing with your ease,
Everyone gasps when you twirl so easily!
"Point your feet," the teacher says,
Little ballerina leaps and leaps,
Little ballerina dances so elegantly,
Her pearly white teeth glimmer in the light,
She dances her heart out in the bright,
Her tutu bounces with every step she makes,
But ballerina misses a step,
Thud!
Will ballerina ever be perfect?
Suddenly her feet lift off the ground,
Ballerina is pirouetting in the air!
As the ballerina's feet slowly hit the ground again,
She slowly bows,
Maybe ballerina is perfect.

Eyoha Tilahun (10)
Mellers Primary School, Radford

Flying High

In my dreams, every night,
Dragons flying high,
Breathing air like a bear,
Watching clowns in the fair,
Unicorns driving one by one, saying, "Hi!"
Dancing fairies in the rainbow sparkling sky,
Getting lost when the stars come by,
Spiders crawling on your eye,
Famous dancers flying high,
The rain spitting from the sky,
We say, "Goodbye."

Rozhin Hamza (10)
Mellers Primary School, Radford

Petals

In my dreams,
I wake up and see,
Nature spreading all around me,
The way the flowers spread and flow,
It's really nice the way they go,
First comes the first trails, then the others,
Waving around like families together,
Flowers here,
And flowers there,
Maybe I'll keep flowers everywhere!

Maram Elemam
Mellers Primary School, Radford

I Like Stars

Blue stars,
Red stars,
Green stars, too.
I like purple stars, how about you?

Orange stars,
Pink stars,
Yellow stars, too.
I like gold stars, how about you?

Maya Kaur
Mellers Primary School, Radford

The Alien On The Moon

In my dreams every night
Astronauts jump high in the space sky
Looking for aliens on the moon
One by one, they looked into a crater
Until one of the astronauts heard a loud noise
They all went to explore the mysterious sound
Suddenly, the alien revealed itself and chased after them
Like a flash, they sprinted back to the rocket ship
And headed back to Earth where there was safety
I sighed in relief until I noticed I was in bed all along.

Arinze Njemanze (11)
St Alfege With St Peter's CE Primary School, Greenwich

The Pitch Of Dreams

In the universe of dreams, a football game starts,
Where cheers and excitement in the atmosphere hold,
The stadium roars with anticipation and glee,
As the teams clash on the pitch, a spectacle to see,
The players with skill and determination in their eyes run and tackle,
Aiming for the winner's prize,
The ball glides through the air, swift and true,
As the crowd held their breath, the tension grew,
With each pass and goal, the energy rose,
The game becomes a symphony of glorious heights,
The roar of the crowd, the thunderous applause,
As the players showcase their talents without a pause,
In this dream, the underdogs rise to the top,
Defying their odds their spirit never drops,
They weave through defenders, swift and agile,
Their teamwork and passion, such an unstoppable style,
The final whistle blows, the dream game concludes,
And the underdogs triumph, their dream is true,
The crowd's celebrations are jubilant and wild,
As dreams and reality merge, a moment to pause,

The pitch is where heroes get noticed and their dreams are truly blessed,
Football is more than just a game,
It's a language spoken in every name.

Obinna Ndukwe (11)
St Alfege With St Peter's CE Primary School, Greenwich

Dreaming About Stickmen

When I start dreaming
Stickmen are running about
Smiles as expressions
Animals walking with their owners
They were always stuck inside my imagination
One day, they started disappearing one by one
I never saw them again
But I know they are out there, somewhere.

Bernice Enadeghe (11)
St Alfege With St Peter's CE Primary School, Greenwich

Dancing Unicorns

I open this door,
And see some unicorns on the floor.
With glittery skirts like the moon,
The music is playing. *Boom! Boom! Boom!*
The disco ball looks like the sun,
Ooh! Those unicorns look like they're having fun.
Shiny confetti in the air,
Dancing unicorns shaking their hair.
My sister's face is shocked like mine,
To see the unicorns having a good time.
A unicorn shouts, "Come and join in!"
We both shout, "Yes!" with a huge, big grin.
My sister grabs my hand and says, "Let's go, go, go!
Dance with me! Dance with me!
Dance with me! Oh! Oh! Oh!"

Marley-Rose Willoughby (6)
St Joseph's RC School, Woodend

Spring Has Sprung

What's here won't disappear,
This smell is now so near,
A fresh breeze all around,
Breathing in new life, we've found.
Colours shining bright and clear,
Making everyone so dear.
Flowers bloom, all in tune,
Silly songs and games play soon.
Lightning under shining sun,
Making memories with everyone.
Stories, rhythms and rhymes,
Fun time in these happy times.
Under rainbows shining above,
Time to rest with those we love.
Tomorrow, we'll play and run,
Under the school day sun.

Wilhemina Fagbohun (7)
St Joseph's RC School, Woodend

Magical Rainbow

S ofia and me, watching the sunset
U p in the shining sky
P ointing at the radiant rainbow
E xcellent unicorns galloping across
R iding through the wonderful rainbows
P anicking because suddenly we see a strong light
O ver it, beaming stars coming towards us
W ondering what it is
E very unicorn receives an extraordinary, remarkable power
R apidly healing someone that is terribly hurt
S inging, rejoicing and we use this new gift.

Maggie Santeugini (7)
St Joseph's RC School, Woodend

My Pokémon Dream And Adventure

In my dreams a tale unfolds,
With Pokémon mates where adventure holds,

Team Rocket spreading fears,
And all the people are in tears,

Dratini is intelligent and wise,
Who is very small in size,

Dragonite's wings are open and wide,
Which are on his side,

I want to win the Pokémon trophy,
And then I will celebrate with toffee.

Arshika Rawat (7)
St Joseph's RC School, Woodend

Far Out...

I look up at the midnight skies,
In between I hear the cries,
Of the stars shooting across the cloudless view,
The Northern Lights are dancing and beaming,
As I carry on dreaming,
The wonders I'm seeing, not always visible to a human being,
I always wonder about the far-out secrets,
I guess they are hidden, or just forbidden,
I look up at the galaxy,
And feel like I am in a gallery,
Full of planets and many wonders,
Where there aren't any thunders,
I look up above, maybe I'll see a dove,
Fluttering into the far out, I look up,
All around me are just memories,
In between I see the worries,
Too much to carry in my head, they once have said,
The Northern Lights are dancing and beaming, as I carry on dreaming,
I imagine the great miracles, though it seems invisible,
Somewhere out there,
Far out...

Natalia Borciuch (10)
St Thomas More's Catholic Primary School, Havant

Superpowers Rule

S uns drop and moons rise,
U nderpants wakes up to make villains meet their demise,
P owers gained and water's shot,
E arly in the morning, Underpants came out of his cot,
R aining city, get ready for him to come,
P owers can make him very dumb,
O lly the Octopus, holder of invisibility,
W ill Underpants defeat him with a useless ability?
E nd of Olly Octopus is now,
R unning over to see his friend, a cow,
S uperpowers rule, now I'm asking you to take a bow.

R ummaging through the rubbish to find lunch,
U nderpants eats and makes a *crunch, munch!*
L oving superhero full of care,
E nding his life for truth or dare.

Olly Sparks (9)
St Thomas More's Catholic Primary School, Havant

A Perfect Dream

Imagine a model living in a city,
Fun, she had,
Her life was pretty,
But behind her rashes,
Her life came down in ashes,
Living in her mansion,
It all came down in crashes,
Her crisp, blonde hair,
And emerald green eyes,
But behind all this,
Was a girl drowning in disguise,
She was only a young lady,
Lost in the blue,
But she felt like she was dying,
And just needed a tissue,
They thought she had a perfect life,
They thought it was outstanding,
But only if they really knew,
The life she really was having,
Some thought she had it easy,
Some thought it was extreme,
But from the outside, all it really looked like,
Was she had the perfect dream.

Enaaya Zeeshan (11)
St Thomas More's Catholic Primary School, Havant

An Endless Nightmare...

All was dark,
People were screaming,
People were shouting,
In the dark abyss below...

Surrounded by darkness, I was here alone,
No one to talk to except for strange creatures I don't know,
Trees curled like fingers, all the way to the sky,
I just had to stay here, until I kissed this world goodbye.

I felt nervous, scared, well it was hard to say,
Whatever I did, I just had to pray,
The last thing I remember, I fell asleep in my castle,
There might have even been a parcel waiting outside my bedroom door...

Whatever this was, it wasn't a dream that holds memories,
It was a nightmare, one that I couldn't get out of...

Jill King (11)
St Thomas More's Catholic Primary School, Havant

Hogwarts Returns

H arry Potter, the one who survived, will go to Hogwarts and thrive,
O nce in Hogwarts, an evil wizard made a blizzard, the one who must not be named was trapped in a frame,
G lad to be in Hogwarts, Harry had new friends and a few pointy ends, but evil was bent,
W hen evil spreads, people lie in beds,
A terrible curse had ended this happy verse,
R eading my mistakes, I don't get any breaks,
T error has ended, I have mended and I'm happy to leave because I am free,
S o I wake up in bed, cuddling my ted and I realise it's a dream instead.

Jessica Barber (10)
St Thomas More's Catholic Primary School, Havant

Untitled

F lags raised as the players walked onto the field,
O ptimism hung high in the air,
O ther players were not on the pitch because they were on the bench,
T eamwork is key in football, they need to work as a team,
B all is the thing that you need to pass around to your team to score a goal,
A player is earning lots of money to play for their team,
L ingering doubts about the fixture weighed on the player's back,
L inesmen are people who run up the pitch to make a decision.

Gabe Fry (10)
St Thomas More's Catholic Primary School, Havant

Nightmares

N othing has prepared me for this horrible fright,
I n the middle of the dark, dark night,
G hosts and vampires all alike,
H ow mean to set my sweet dreams alight,
T *hud!* Suddenly a big, loud noise,
M ake way, here come my creepy toys,
"A ttack!" yells Twister, head of the plastic,
R oary just says, "This is fantastic,"
E erie eyes glow, as I close my own,
S uddenly, I wake up to find I'm safe at home in bed.

Alice Bates (10)
St Thomas More's Catholic Primary School, Havant

Nightmares

N othing for me in this strange wood I see.
I take a tiptoe forward as nervous as can be.
G lancing all around all I see is smoke.
H ow did I get in this haze? Must be a joke.
T *hud! Smash!* Something crumbles around me.
M y terrifying fear is shown - a spooky, petrifying clown.
A m I lost?
R ip the cost.
E erie eyes glow, and I close my own in creepy dread.
S oon enough, I wake up to find I'm safe at home in bed!

Eden Ross (10)
St Thomas More's Catholic Primary School, Havant

Once Upon A Dream

Once upon a dream,
A wizard was once seen,
Causing chaos conjuring magic,
Making quite a scene,
Many survived but struggled to thrive,
No one was overly keen.

Once upon a dream,
Pirate ships did gleam,
Striking gold would soon take its toll,
With loot and leisure around.

Once upon a dream,
A creamy trifle treat,
I gobbled it up,
It went in my gut,
To be belched back up,
I think I got the unlucky nut!

Matthew Dixon (10)
St Thomas More's Catholic Primary School, Havant

The Royal Pirates

R oyal Pirate I may be,
O n day two,
Y ou'll notice very strange things about me,
A pirate with a hook and sword,
L ooks like a monster but well may be,

P eculiar is he,
I wonder what it may be,
R uby-red hair, but glee,
A t last, I'm at sea,
T ime is ticking,
E xtravaganza, you may see,
S o at last, you may see... peculiar things about me.

Maddison Sutton (10)
St Thomas More's Catholic Primary School, Havant

Football

There are many different sports in the world,
Tennis,
Basketball,
Hockey,
And so much more,
But the best of them all is,
Football,
It may seem rough,
Although it may be tough,
It's my passion,
Along with its good fashion,
So come and join me,
And we shall be,
People who we are meant to be,
Don't worry, I'll be there too,
With you,
Just remember,
You can join in September.

Millie Wilson (11)
St Thomas More's Catholic Primary School, Havant

Arsenal Are The Best

A rsenal are the best
R unning through the games
S coring all the goals with mighty Havertz
E verything is easy when you've got Rice
N orth London forever
A rsenal you are The Gunners destroying them on the pitch
L osers are from Man City

F ootball is their life
C ome with me and you'll see that Arsenal are going to win the Premier League.

Elliott Boyce (9)
St Thomas More's Catholic Primary School, Havant

Friendly Monster

The friendly monster appears in my dreams at night,
But the fur on his back isn't so bright.
Although he seems quite big and scary,
He is actually just big and friendly.
I go to bed and in my dreams,
There he is again, but not as scary as it seems.
I went outside and walked on the crunchy leaves,
And he followed behind and asked to play with me.

Anya Gohil (10)
St Thomas More's Catholic Primary School, Havant

Football

F antastic players skill across the pitch.
O ver the pitch was a bird,
O ver all of the players.
T o top it off, it looked special,
B ecause it had rainbow wings.
A ll of the fans didn't notice it.
L uxurious flow across the pitch.
L uckily the commentators noticed it.

Alfie Anderson (9)
St Thomas More's Catholic Primary School, Havant

The Magical Land

Suddenly, I saw magical stars glistening in the night and they gave off a magical light. It was a dream world with a divine sheet made out of cotton. It was like I fell out of the world into a mysterious comfy paradise. I was so zoned in, I didn't need to be with anyone. I felt so relaxed, so I fell asleep for two days and then I felt so energised.

Dexter Johnson (10)
St Thomas More's Catholic Primary School, Havant

Cricket

C ricket can be a sport,
R ight-handed batter and bowler,
I don't like left-handed batters and bowlers,
C ricket can be a sport or a nought for you,
K icking a ball is football but bowling is cricket,
E xcept there are some rules,
T here is one sport in particular, cricket.

Bella Swales (10)
St Thomas More's Catholic Primary School, Havant

Sugar Rush

Once upon a dream,
In the land of ice cream,
There are a lot of flavours you can desire,
But just be careful, for you might start a fire.

Your human friends will get angry,
Or worse, hangry,
You have a lot of powers,
To clean it up.

Don't eat too much,
'Cause you might throw up!

Andrew Mitchell (10), Felix Linto & Freddie
St Thomas More's Catholic Primary School, Havant

Anime

Made in Japan,
As cute as a pea,
Anime is watched on TV.
From spirits, to witches, to normal,
From eggs, to something formal.
Pirates sailing across the sea.
Witches flying above me.
Vampires and humans.
The fire burns.
In the flick of a wand,
Anime and me have a bond.

Nellie Goudarzi (11)
St Thomas More's Catholic Primary School, Havant

My Nightmare...

I couldn't see anything in the dark, empty room,
All I could hear was a sweep of a broom,
I tried to scream, but no one could hear me,
I could only just about see,
I saw glowing, red eyes,
A manic grin spread across its sinister face,
Where am I?
The only possible explanation is... my dream.

Elsie Stouse (10)
St Thomas More's Catholic Primary School, Havant

The Night

The creeps follow you everywhere,
You can see them through the window,
The dreaded creatures want you dead,
Not right as the midnight bell strikes,
You block up everything in sight,
You trace every track of the unseen,
As morning comes, there is nothing left,
But a dead body on the floor.

Andrew Wardon (10)
St Thomas More's Catholic Primary School, Havant

Dragons

D ragons are my favourite reptile,
R ather they are filled with denial,
A nd they can breathe fire,
G reen ones aren't easy to acquire,
O n the mountains, you will see,
N o dragons appear on the sea,
S o look carefully at the mountain peak.

Caiden Aylett (10)
St Thomas More's Catholic Primary School, Havant

Duel

As the tumbleweed blows
And the sunlight glows
Gunshots fire as duels commence

Sunset goes
Night rises
Midnight sounds creep in the night

3, 2, 1... Fire

One dead, one alive

That's how it goes.

Lenny Tyler (10)
St Thomas More's Catholic Primary School, Havant

Clowns

I hate clowns.
They're my worst nightmare.
I think they're under my bed at night.
I'm too scared to look under, just in case they're there.
Oh, why do I have a fear of them?
They're harmless, right?

Alarna Gomez (10)
St Thomas More's Catholic Primary School, Havant

Magic Rainbow

M ake
A
G iant
I n
C reation

R ed
A lphabet
I nvention
N o
B ones
O n
W ord, just lemon curd.

Niamh Haynes (11)
St Thomas More's Catholic Primary School, Havant

Mother's Crimes

Once upon a time, I always had to fight for my mother's crimes
And I had to admit that I did it this whole time
Because I had my mother's gem
And everyone called me Rose Quartz.

Artur Eva (10)
St Thomas More's Catholic Primary School, Havant

A Bat With A Hat Meets A Spider

A bove the caves, there was a…

B at with a hat and he complained
A nd an ant was not a very good friend
T hen he thought of an animal to be

W ith. First, he thought of an
I nsect, like a ladybug but
T hen he thought of a spider
H e looked around for a spider

A nd there was no sign of it

H e found it but after half
A n hour, he found a spider
T hen he came up to him

& said hi, he did not respond

A nd then he said hi, the bat

S aid, "Come on, I will show you around."
"**P** lease," the bat said.
"**I** can go and no one else."
"**D** o you have a friend?" said the
E nchanting spider. "Yes, but I'm looking for someone to do
R eading with me." The spider said, "Yes, on you, to be."

Alan Sowa (8)
White Meadows Primary School, Wick

Candy World

I'm lost in a dream, I might even scream,
I am floating around, suddenly, I touch the ground.
I look up and see a candy world, who could ever be this free?
Somebody comes up to me, it is a chocolate lady!
She greets me and says, "No one in this candy world goes to bed!"
All of a sudden, an evil and mean jellyfish appears from the underground, and makes the air swish round and round.
I take it upon myself to save the kingdom, the candy cane king says, "Oh no, I'll lose all my brocolates and belfs."

Brocolates and belfs are not what you think,
They are a fancy drink, and something called brink.

In the blink of an eye, the cruel jellyfish was gone, by everyone working together,
I hope this poem gets passed on forever and ever!
My fluffy pet was the hero, now I want to be a vet!

Bethany Fenner (8)
White Meadows Primary School, Wick

Space Adventure

S pace and stars shining
P arts of me were amazed
A tiny star made friends
"**C** ome and play with me," she said
"**E** rr okay," I said. "Why?

A nd what's your name?"
"**D** elilah, because my mum said Delilah is special."
"**V** ery nice, I love that name."
"**E** rr, what happened to that star?" said Delilah
"**N** ot again," I said. A bunch of stars were
 T urning black, so we set off to see what happened
 U ttering and muttering in the journey through
 R omance Planet and Candy Planet, delicious! Then
 E verywhere we looked, black there was. But a trigger was pulled to make stars angry. Suddenly, all the stars were happy again.

Harriette Talman (7)
White Meadows Primary School, Wick

The Best Olympics

T he crowd goes wild,
H ere comes Simone Biles, the best Olympic gymnast.
E veryone cheers for her.

B ecause she is going to do the best gymnastics,
E very time she is doing something, people cheer.
S ometimes, she might make a mistake, but don't worry,
T he best gymnast in the world doesn't make them often.

O ne day, people might hurt themselves,
L uckily, not all the time!
Y ou are the best,
M agnificent Simone.
P aige, you are next up to perform,
I felt so scared to perform at the Olympics!
"**C** ome on, Paige," said Simone. "Good luck!"
S uddenly, I woke up and I was in bed.

Paige Skinner (8)
White Meadows Primary School, Wick

Space Horse And Fun In The Candy World

Something wasn't right when I peeped into the room and saw Precious. A gorgeous white horse in the room that looked scared and terrified. I tried to understand what the horse was saying, but it gave me a letter saying, "Hello, my name is Sparkle and who are you?" "My name is Holly," I said. "What do you like to do for fun?"
"I like to go to space and explore," Sparkle explained.
It was getting late. As we were sleeping, a fairy came and said a spell to make the horse's dream come true. She said, "Abracadabra." And then we were teleported up into space.
We woke up and were surprised to see Mars, the horse's favourite. The next day, we were at Candy World, my favourite.

Lyna Ben Amor (8)
White Meadows Primary School, Wick

A Big House

Once upon a time, there was a big house in a lonely country. But suddenly, a red car was coming in the distance. A little girl lived in the house. In the little red car, sat a little boy.

When he arrived at the house, he said, "I wish you were mine."

She said, "What's your name?"

He said, "Ocean."

"Well," she said, "do you want a cup of tea?"

"No, thank you," he said.

So they got married and had children, five were boys and five were girls. Unfortunately, the little girl's mummy had passed away. The family were so sad, they did not go to the funeral. The family was okay from then.

Marlie Winter (8)
White Meadows Primary School, Wick

The World Of Wonder And Anything

As I step onto the cloud,
Donald my duck is loud,
I turn around to pick him up,
But whoosh! There is a blank space.
I forgot anything can happen,
I've now lost my companion,
And then I start to levitate,
50 stars are underneath me,
They take me to a rainbow of unicorns,
I hop on one and wish me luck,
Me and my unicorn soar through the sky,
How lucky I am to get dropped next to a pond,
My little Donald swims back to me,
It's like he felt my presence,
I'm happy to be with him now,
The world of wonder isn't very wonderful after all.

Mylee-Jayne Legge (8)
White Meadows Primary School, Wick

The Girl Who Was Brave

Once upon a time, there was a girl who was a fairy. Her name was Vanellope. She was brave. She was an athlete.

Her mother was very sick so the little girl went to the shop. She didn't know that the Candy Land Clown had come back. She bought the medicine and turned around and screamed. The clown started to chase her all the way home!

Suddenly, her fairy godmother appeared and sent the clown back to prison. The clown saw a baby dragon riding a unicorn.

Vanellope went home and gave her mum the medicine. A few weeks later she was better, and they lived happily ever after.

Vanellope Yardley (8)
White Meadows Primary School, Wick

A World Of Superpowers

Once upon a time, I walked into a rainbow door and was amazed by what I saw. There were all my favourite animals. They all ran towards me and then I found my pet, a dog.
He turned and licked my face. Then me and my dog fell down a hole, but then I stopped falling. I flew to the top, but my dog disappeared. I saw him in front of a house.
I flew my way there, but he walked inside and I saw my favourite animal, an axolotl in a fish tank. It was swimming around happily and then, *whoosh!* It swam out of the tank, and then I closed my eyes and I was in my bed.

Eliza Cranham (8)
White Meadows Primary School, Wick

A Superstitious Fog

A magic world unites
You and me
It is big, small, all sizes
All in one, us, light, dark
And neither!
A beautiful night was set
A light, flaming in beauty
Which made a new race
My dad fought in a
Great war, fatal attacks
Rain some more
Death awaits any age
My world then adapted
Into a great one, he was indeed
But not all was good
As a cloudy fog
Was released, killing thousands
And awakening dragons
Outraged
Now I say, "Beware!"

Dexter Taylor (8)
White Meadows Primary School, Wick

The Pitch Invader

Here I go to the football match
Watching my idol Mbappé
1-0 down, but we're not giving up
I ran down onto the pitch
I scored a free kick
I outran the security
Someone helped me up
I didn't get hurt
So I didn't get banned from the stadium
I just noticed Mbappé signed my kit when I threw my kit at him
I watched the rest of the match
PSG won 2-4
It was the best day of my life
I just noticed that my friend Caelan filmed me.

Jake Blackwell (8)
White Meadows Primary School, Wick

Hair

H airy people come into the salon
A bove the roof are seagulls, eating bread and making a nest
I ndependent hairdresser
R ound the hair
D irty people but when they come out, they look nice
R unning my fingers through their hair
E ach and every person in the town comes to the salon
S alon is beautiful
S urely this girl is alive
E at in here but away from the equipment
R eply to me if it is good.

Ruby James (8)
White Meadows Primary School, Wick

The Big Match!

Maya, Paja and Ari,
Were practising playing football in Bali,
Maya scored 6 goals and 1 penalty,
While Paja and Ari cheered happily,
A few years later,
Something was greater,
Maya, Paja and Ari,
Played an actual match in Bali,
They won,
And had lots of fun!
Then they met a bunch of famous football players,
Even there, lots of people were higher than them by layers,
Maya, Paja and Ari were very successful,
Especially Maya, she was very joyful!

Isra Kamali (8)
White Meadows Primary School, Wick

Fairyland

Once upon a time, there lived some fairies, and they felt alone. Their fairy queen told them to have some fun, but they still felt alone.
"What can we do?" said Ruby.
Then all of a sudden, a person appeared out of nowhere! Her name was Violet. First, she asked where she was. The fairies said Fairyland. They played all day until it was time for Violet to go.
The fairies said, "Bye Violet," and the fairies never forgot that memory.

Violet Baker (8)
White Meadows Primary School, Wick

Nightmares

N o one told me where I could be
I t's too dark to even see
G oing forward, I see a light
H owever, it's getting bright
T he light goes out, I see a cloud
M y heart is beating, it's kinda loud
A m I crazy, or is that a clown?
R unning away, I see my bed
E yes glow, they look red
S uddenly, I wake up in my cosy bed, finally it's the end.

Elise Wheatley (8)
White Meadows Primary School, Wick

Getting Lost

In my dreams, me and my mum went to the jungle. Once we got in we signed in and saw some giraffes and monkeys. We had an expert to keep us safe. Whilst we were walking I saw my favourite animal, a zebra and when I looked back they were gone. I was panicking, I couldn't find them anywhere. So I checked the front of the jungle. After I checked the front of the jungle, 5 minutes later, I woke up and was laughing and woke my mum up.

Ivy-Grace Patridge (8)
White Meadows Primary School, Wick

Mystical Glider

Every night I drift off to sleep and dream of flying in the sky. Flying past clouds made of cotton candy. Far away lies my home in a secret dome.
As I get home I hop across the clouds watching unicorns fly by. I glide past them and reach the highest point and know I have gone the wrong way. I cross the surface to explore until I come across an unknown castle.
Who knows where I will go?

Hannah Man (8)
White Meadows Primary School, Wick

Getting Lost

One day, a mysterious door turned up and I went in. I saw dragons flying and breathing fire. The creepy thing was that I was alone, yes that's right, I was alone.
But suddenly, I started to levitate and I was even more scared. The worst thing was it was very dark and then it was time to escape this dream.
But wait, there was an exit which I went through.
Yay, I was home!

Lilly Doyle (8)
White Meadows Primary School, Wick

What Can I Do With This Creature?

M ost people are scared but something happened
O ne time, a twenty-armed creature chased me
N o one was there
S ee, I see a box, so I went in it to hide
T racking the monster uses its smell to find me
E ntering the box and I'm scared
R un but it was a trap, the monster was there.

Kian Wolfe (8)
White Meadows Primary School, Wick

The Fantasy World!

I hope my dream shall come true,
Just like I drew,
Pixies flying and prancing around,
As the rainbow crops grow in the ground,
Just like a dragon roaring his fiery breath,
But to be careful you don't want to meet your death,
And here I am meeting a fairy,
But she was quite glary,
As I wished, I said goodbye.

Matylda Beaumont (7)
White Meadows Primary School, Wick

I Wish I Was A Trillionaire

I wish I was a trillionaire
Who helps the poor and poorly people
When I see someone sick
I would help them
And give them a home to live in
I live in a mansion
Which has a boat and a garden
And is the happiest place in the world
It makes people happy
When everyone is joyless and sad.

Jacob Elijah Thayre (7)
White Meadows Primary School, Wick

Footballer

F ootball is in front of me
O h, what do I do?
O h well, score of course!
T he goal is in front of me
B ut I hit the bar
A ll hope is lost
L ook around, cheering, wait what? It went in!
"**L** et's go!" I shout.

Caelan Barton (8)
White Meadows Primary School, Wick

The Naughty Little Fairy

The naughty little fairy would make sure everyone was asleep and if a child wasn't asleep she would pull one of their teeth out.
She liked everyone asleep because she didn't want to be caught by people or frighten them with her tiny face because she had already frightened too many people.

Nyah Shereni (8)
White Meadows Primary School, Wick

Penguins

P recious friends that I made
E vie is the penguin that found me
N ever give up
G o into the town hall
U nder the stars
I n there I became emperor
"N o way," I said
S o that is why penguins are the best.

Holly Benson (8)
White Meadows Primary School, Wick

Untitled

Football legend, best on the pitch,
Always have the ball and score every goal,
Never give up, always hard work,
Every day, in all weather,
Never lose the ball because I am a legend,
So no one tackles me so it is easy and I will never miss a shot.

Lewis Ross Hardy (8)
White Meadows Primary School, Wick

Heaven, The Best

H ell is terrible while I shine,
E ven my friends agree,
A lso, I'm the King of Heaven,
V ery, so set foot in my magical kingdom,
E very step is another friend,
N o one is mean in my kingdom.

Jacob Lucas (8)
White Meadows Primary School, Wick

Pandas Flying About

P andas are starting to rule
A bove, they look cool and drool
N othing will ever stop them
D o care, the leader has an emerald gem
A round the clouds, they relax
S cour around for their facts.

Siyana Todorova (8)
White Meadows Primary School, Wick

Untitled

F abulous, pretty, famous,
A mazingly pretty best friend,
M ore pretty than usual,
O ver there is a girl too beautiful to be alive,
U sed to be mean,
S o pretty it could kill you.

Ivy Martin (8)
White Meadows Primary School, Wick

Untitled

D reary, scary, mean
R ude, unkind, animal
A ctually a dancer
G reen camouflage
O bviously bad
N o questions about me
S o scary, I could kill you.

Ava Misselbrook (8)
White Meadows Primary School, Wick

Untitled

When I was strolling through the forest, I saw a dog. When I stepped a little bit closer to the suspicious dog, I turned into the dog and my friend Jake was with me. I felt very soft and weird and I instantly died.

Ollie Williamson (7)
White Meadows Primary School, Wick

Untitled

In my dreams this is what happened at the show,
At first the show was going great,
Until it got messed up by a boy called Nate,
He ruined it and made it bad,
It made everybody mad.

Kaitlyn Akers (8)
White Meadows Primary School, Wick

Wizard

W ings are on
I n the cat
Z ebra running in
A potion creating
R eading wizard books, every book read
D one all the spells.

Albi Taylor (8)
White Meadows Primary School, Wick

Tennis Competition

We did some practice tennis to be ready for the competition. The competition started now and my team won a trophy. And at the end of the competition, we had a party and food.

Latisha Banson (8)
White Meadows Primary School, Wick

Untitled

In my dream, I am the world's famous party girl and have really good friends like Ivy-Grace and Scarlett and I live in a giant castle and get to wear fancy dresses.

Nova-Grace Harding (7)
White Meadows Primary School, Wick

Play With Pele And Ronaldo

Once upon a dream, I played football with Pele and Ronaldo at Old Trafford. And when I scored, Pele and Ronaldo gave me two of their rarest boots in the world.

Ronnie Hodder (8)
White Meadows Primary School, Wick

Boxing

B ox him up
O n the ground
X -ray, he had an X-ray
I won
N ight-time he was bitter
G ood win.

Logan Lamb-Gardner (8)
White Meadows Primary School, Wick

Football

F avourite
O n and
O ff
T he
B all
A lways
L oving
L ife.

Junior Kerse (8)
White Meadows Primary School, Wick

A Life Of Richness

As I lie in my cosy, luxurious, fluffy bed, the sun shines through the rich, long curtains that hang from a silver, shiny, metal bar.
As I read my book about rich people, it is getting windy and the brown, sharp trees are roaring like a dinosaur. After reading my book, I need some fresh air, so I put my head out the window and see two nice people walking across the silver, clear, shiny path the colour of a dolphin. I hear a creaky sound in the forest and I see a tall, sharp tree about to fall over because it is wobbling like a penguin.
Somewhere in the distance, a fluffy, white, creamy bird jumps onto the tree, then, *bang!* Leaves fall onto the floor, but the bird luckily gets away.
But I'm here. Safe, in my cosy, luxurious, tall, pretty house.

Jesse Wye (9)
William Martin CE Junior School, Harlow

A Gloomy Forest Day

The gloomy forest was peacefully resting until I came,
Running backwards and forwards in the cool breeze,
Vast, thick trees were observing their surroundings with their crunchy ears,
And, slowly falling asleep in only a couple of minutes,
I finally found it: the colossal hillside,
I celebrated by throwing some crunchy autumn leaves high up in the whistling air,
As I climbed up the colossal hill, the cool breeze punched my skin
While it shouted all of its dark and intriguing secrets,
When I hit the top of the colossal hill, the wind avoided me,
I quickly slid down the relaxing hillside as I said my final goodbyes.

Jacob Adams (9)
William Martin CE Junior School, Harlow

The Abandoned House In The Scary Woods

As I walk closer to the eerie abandoned house,
I hear trees whispering, branches falling,
It is hard to dodge them,
The trees are so close together, like a solid brick wall,
The house is a footstep away,
Whoosh! Shadows zoom past, I jump,
The pitch-black sky with fluffy, grey clouds like children,
I am nervous.
Somewhere in the distance, I hear crows cawing,
The door is there, I reach out,
The handle is as cold as ice,
I turn it slowly,
Shaking from head to toe with fear,
Ring, goes my alarm,
It is all a dream.

Jack Hogg (9)
William Martin CE Junior School, Harlow

An Amazing Ride

As I sit on my comfy bright yellow chair, I look up to the bright blinding sun. When I look down the sun shines across the sunny stones. The nearby grass looks like it is feeling hot but lying there is a vegetable garden. All the vegetables are fully grown healthily.
In the sky, I can see fluffy white clouds jumping over each other slowly. I hear the whooshing air come towards me.
Somewhere in the distance is a big apple tree until, *crash!* The apple tree starts to dislodge and loosen from the cliff, shaking it down. But here I am, sitting comfortably at the top.

Leo Rees (8)
William Martin CE Junior School, Harlow

A Noisy Day At The Funfair

As I arrived at the noisy funfair, the wind roared like a tiger roaring for food! Kids were running with excitement, like a fast cheetah running to eat an animal for its lunch.

The sun shone like gold glitter, shining like a star. Somewhere in the distance, a noisy seagull was taking a sandwich. *Snap!*

I was watching like an audience watching a movie. Children ran forwards, backwards, forwards, backwards.

Suddenly, there was a *bang!* With panting breath, I opened my eyes, happy to realise I was still lying in my soft, comfy bed.

Ajla Hoxha (9)
William Martin CE Junior School, Harlow

A Magical Amusement Park

As you step foot into this amusement park, you'll notice this is no ordinary park,
There is fun and excitement filling the air,
There are rides as colossal as a field,
There are millions of rides that are beyond human sight,
Screech, bang, crash fills the ears as roller coasters screech and racing cars crash,
There are ridiculous rides that go lightning-fast speeds,
Rainbows fill the crystal blue sky,
Children yelling as the rides begin,
Birds tweeting as humans laugh.

Liban Ahmed (9)
William Martin CE Junior School, Harlow

A Day At The Beach

As I lie on the soft golden sand,
The sun smiles at the sea,
The sea watching kids playing with the golden sand,
Like an audience watching a play,
In the sunny, crystal sky, sun looking at the soft sand,
I hear the children laugh as they splash water from the sea,
Somewhere in the distance, an annoying voice says,
"Buy water because it is too hot" before I hear a snap,
It is the glasses breaking on the sand,
But I'm here, lying on the soft golden sand.

Eliana Patti (9)
William Martin CE Junior School, Harlow

Abandoned Amusement Park

As I stepped into the eerie, dark, abandoned amusement park
The stars shone their bright light on the towering trees
The colossal walls beamed down silently like the Queen's royal guards
In the shadowy dark night sky, clouds tried to cover the gloomy night moon
I heard the creak of doors
Swinging back and forward, back and forward
Somewhere in the distance, I heard a scary scream before, *boom!*
A tree fell down
But I was here, safe in the silent building.

Spencer Matthews (9)
William Martin CE Junior School, Harlow

The Castle Of Food

My castle is made of sweet custard creams,
With the finest edges of chocolate ice cream.
The doors of Crunchie bars and pillows of cotton candy.
The roof tiles are made from creamy chocolate bars.
When it's sunny, my castle smells like fresh scones straight out of the oven.
Often, I hear a *drip, drip, drip* but it's just Sprite coming out of the tap.
Sometimes I hear a *bang*!
But don't worry, it's just the bubblegum balloons popping.

Naomi Woodley (9)
William Martin CE Junior School, Harlow

A Day At The Beach

As I lie on my warm, soft deck chair,
The bright sun beams and shines at the sand,
The sun is watching the playful children play like a show,
In the bright, blue, crystal sky,
Clouds are waving like cotton candy.

I hear the giggling of children jumping,
Waves across and across and across the sand in the distance,
Somewhere in the distance, I hear a seagull snatching another doughnut,
But I am here, lying on my warm, soft deck chair.

Max Cuthbert (9)
William Martin CE Junior School, Harlow

My Beautiful Treehouse

My beautiful treehouse is made out of grass,
With a natural-coloured, rocky spire,
Healthy, juicy and yummy fruit roof tiles,
And a beautiful door full of exotic flowers,
When it's very sunny, my treehouse smells as beautiful as roses,
Its lovely chimney reaches up to the sky,
And sometimes, I hear my treehouse drip,
Occasionally I hear my tree house go *bang!*
No need to worry, it's somewhere from the lightbulbs popping.

Filip Piziorski (9)
William Martin CE Junior School, Harlow

A Day On A Sunny Beach

As I walk on a warm, delightful beach,
The sunlight beams on the golden sand,
The children laugh like funny hyenas giggling,
In the sapphire blue sky, the fluffy snow-white clouds,
I hear the waves crashing together like a massive argument.
Somewhere in the distance, a crash from the waves hitting together,
A warning before *bang*! The ocean gets angry,
But I'm here, standing on a warm, delightful beach.

Louie Brandle (9)
William Martin CE Junior School, Harlow

A Life In Space

Space World always moves around, and the sky is as dark as night.
The floor is made of unbreakable glass, and the sky spirits fly away.
The wind moves smoothly from left to right, and the stars warm the night.
Platforms as soft as pillow fluff elevate low and high.
The gardens are blue like crystal light, and the water tastes like cotton candy.
The houses are as neat as fantastic heaven and it's a great, wonderful night.

Muhammad Khalid Ibrahim (9)
William Martin CE Junior School, Harlow

The Dark Forest

As I walk into a gloomy, eerie forest,
The dark trees whisper secrets far and wide,
The soundless sky watches like a cat looking for its prey,
The dark, green leaves listen to a nearby river flowing gently,
I can hear birds saying goodnight to each other,
Somewhere in the distance, a mysterious wolf howls as *crash!*
A branch falls close to it.
But I am here at the entrance of the dark, frightening forest.

Helena Ingall (9)
William Martin CE Junior School, Harlow

Mysterious Space

Comets shatter through space at 82 mph,
Every second a star is born.

Saturn's rings are like being at the seaside,
Kapow, crash, bang,
Don't worry, it's only Mars' volcanoes.

Black holes consume anything in their way,
The sun is the only light in space.

Surprisingly, we're not alone,
There are trillions of galaxies.

Ben Hollis (9)
William Martin CE Junior School, Harlow

A Winter Wonderland

Snowflakes as blue as the sea.
Clouds as white as snow.
Foxes as warm as the sun.
Lakes as frozen as thick ice.
People ice skating like dancers doing a performance.
Stars shining as bright as the moon, auras as neon as a rainbow.
Skies as dark as a black hole.
Fireworks as bright as a star.
Fire explodes as fast as light.
The moon as radiant as lightning.

Malakai Oderinde (9)
William Martin CE Junior School, Harlow

Lionel Messi

As the magical footballer walked out of the tunnel,
Messi waved and gave them a giggle,
As his crystal blue kit shined in the bright yellow sun,
When everyone got louder and louder,
As they started the game, Messi had a chance, and the crowd went wild,
Messi got man of the match,
In the end, it was 2-2 to Messi.

Ellie Williamson (8)
William Martin CE Junior School, Harlow

The Dream Of The Universe

The dimness of space swallowed the spaceship whole,
The stars gleamed smiling at the spaceship,
As fast as a flash the engine went full power,
I landed on a magical planet and ventured out in my snow-white suit,
The planet was rocky and full of mountains,
I launched back home,
Was it a dream or was it reality?

Stanley Gibb (9)
William Martin CE Junior School, Harlow

The Beach

Lying on the gold sand, children swimming with joy,
Adults chilling in the warm weather.

People building gold sandcastles,
Dolphins jumping up and down in the crystal sea like a trampoline.

Adults drinking cold drinks in the shade,
Slurp, slurp!

Cavell Brefo-Anum (9)
William Martin CE Junior School, Harlow

The Sky

I was floating like a bird in the sky.
The rainbow Earth under me was beautiful.
When the rain came down, *drip*, *drip* it went.
My dream swallowed me up into a hole.
The cloud was as soft as a feather.
The sky was as blue as sapphires.

Joseph Didcock (9)
William Martin CE Junior School, Harlow

The Savannah Plains

The plains, full of interesting wildlife,
Many species live there,
Golden lions,
Roaring like a raging cat,
Big grey elephants,
With their long trunks,
Sucking up water from the pool,
Black feathery ostriches,
Grazing in flocks.

George Doyle-Worton (9)
William Martin CE Junior School, Harlow

The Colourful World Below

Last night I had a dream.
As I float in the sky
I realise
The world below
Is as beautiful as a rainbow.
As the clouds swallow me whole
Bang! I land on my feet.
I realise that, now, I'm on the world below.

Brody Wayman (9)
William Martin CE Junior School, Harlow

The Seaside

The sun ran across the sand. The clouds whispered across the beach. The waves crashed across the sand. The club leader smiled at you when you sat under it. Sunglasses smile at the sun and the sun will smile back.

Braxton Findlay (9)
William Martin CE Junior School, Harlow

The Kittens Filled With Questions

What's my name?
You call me Fuzzy,
You call me Kitty,
You call me Cutie,
You call me Fuzzball,
And now you call me Timmy,
6 little kittens, sitting in a basket,
Full of tears and nothing to make it,
One by one they disappear, this is their worst fear,
Losing each other,
To live in a new home,
Family, a new mummy to love,
A new life to live and to roam,
They come in sizes, big and small,
Fluffy and rough,
They keep themselves to themselves,
I don't know what I would do without the world's best animals, cats.

Ellie-Lou Simpson (10)
Willow Wood Community Primary, Wharton

Luigi's Ghostly Journey

In Luigi's mansion, where darkness finds its throne,
Echoes of forgotten tales, in whispers groan.
In every shadowed corner, secrets dwell,
Within the walls where ghostly spectres swell.
Yet, Luigi strides, his courage underrated,
Through the halls, where shadows dance, by fear unstirred.
But little does he know, a greater mystery awaits,
In the heart of the mansion, where darkness dictates.

Damien Durose (10)
Willow Wood Community Primary, Wharton

The Day I Flew

The sky was grey, it was a miserable day,
It was raining, so I couldn't go out to play,
I was brushing my teeth when I noticed a bottle,
The label read, 'How to fly'. I was startled.
As quick as a flash, I drank it all,
This has been my dream since I was young!
No sooner than I had drunk it, I felt a bit sick,
I wished I hadn't drunk all of it!
Suddenly, as quick as lightning, I shot up onto the roof,
Crash!
I soared in the air, as wild as a bear!
I shot across the rooftops, house to house,
The streets were silent, as quiet as a mouse,
I soon realised that nobody knew,
I wanted to get up to mischief too!
I ate all the sweets from the newsagent's shop,
I flew to Big Ben, right to the very top!
Then I went to the swimming pool,
Mum said, "Wake up, you're late for school!"

Sophia Davis (9)
Wilmslow Preparatory School, Wilmslow

I Lost My Work

On Tuesday night, in the twilight,
I dreamt about my school,
"I'm so sorry, Teacher,
I dropped my work inside my pool!
I tried to get it out,
But my dog swallowed it in the pool!
You won't believe what I say,
It all sounds like nonsense!
My dog grew wings,
And flew away like a rocket,
Without a trace!
It landed on Mars,
And will be stranded forever,
Like my cat Charles!
I don't expect you to believe any of what I've said."
My teacher was furious!
He grew sharp claws and beady eyes,
I screamed in fear and prayed for my life,
But it was all a dream!
I am safe after all,
And anyway, I only have a cat.

William Teahan (9)
Wilmslow Preparatory School, Wilmslow

Elemental Superpowers

Wizards came upon this land.
There they went to protect with their powers, there once came another threat, made of emerald green.
We started shaking with fear, could they do it next?
I suddenly felt power through my body.
I felt elemental.
I finally laughed with glee, I looked fierce like the lion I was.
I could use the powers of Poseidon, Zeus, land and Earth.
So the emerald-green figure trembled with fear, it jumped over a river going up as fast as a cheetah.
Then I suddenly felt like me again,
I went back to normal, they cheered me with happiness,
I was a hero.

William Lambert (8)
Wilmslow Preparatory School, Wilmslow

The Horse From The Sky

When I dream each night
I sit up in bed
To wait for my horse from the sky
I sprinkle the glitter
The glitter from space
Then my horse from the sky will come galloping
Across the dark, midnight, black, blue sky
Rainbows kicking from its hooves
As I jump aboard onto her silky back
As black as the trees
In the deep, dark forest
Houses and the small village turn from lifelike to
Toy doll houses
As we gallop across the sky
My friends appear and all of my worries float
Away
And melt into
Dust.

Ava Ummat (9)
Wilmslow Preparatory School, Wilmslow

Oceans

In the world of oceans,
Dolphins splash up from the
Colourful, turquoise ocean.
Sharks hunt for delicious fish
In the sparkling blue ocean.
Fish swim as speedily
As they can swim
Away from being eaten
By the scary, blue shark!
Seahorses in the indigo-blue ocean
Swim side to side like
A person who doesn't know
How to drive,
Goldfish are swimming happily.
Suddenly, I am back in my
Cosy bed!

Cailey Li (8)
Wilmslow Preparatory School, Wilmslow

Dancing In The Clouds

Tonight I shall dream up in the sky,
Dancing on rainbows, up I will fly,
Unicorns, fairies, creatures galore,
Clouds like cotton candy on which I will soar,
Ecstatic and graceful, I dance through the sky,
And the magical creatures watch me swoop by,
Sadly, a unicorn swoops me back into my bed,
Thinking of my wonderful dream in my head.

Molly McConville (8)
Wilmslow Preparatory School, Wilmslow

YoungWriters® Est. 1991

YOUNG WRITERS INFORMATION

We hope you have enjoyed reading this book – and that you will continue to in the coming years.

If you're a young writer who enjoys reading and creative writing, or the parent of an enthusiastic poet or story writer, do visit our website **www.youngwriters.co.uk**. Here you will find free competitions, workshops and games, as well as recommended reads, a poetry glossary and our blog.

If you would like to order further copies of this book, or any of our other titles, then please give us a call or visit **www.youngwriters.co.uk**.

Young Writers
Remus House
Coltsfoot Drive
Peterborough
PE2 9BF
(01733) 890066
info@youngwriters.co.uk

 YoungWritersUK   YoungWritersCW
 youngwriterscw   youngwriterscw